THE PAIN BEHIND THE FLESH

SURVIVING THE WOUNDS NO ONE COULD SEE

DOMINICK TICE

This is a work of nonfiction. The events and reflections described are based on the author's personal experiences and memories. Some names and identifying details have been changed to protect the privacy of individuals.

The author is not a licensed therapist, counselor, or medical professional. This book is intended as a personal testimony and should not be used as a substitute for professional mental health treatment or medical advice. If you are struggling, please seek support from a qualified professional.

Published by: Echo and Hope Publishing

Book cover design by: Bojan Rekovic

Edited by: Dr. Vivian Cockrell

ISBN: 979-8-99374400-1

Disclaimer / Content Warning

This book tells my story the way I lived it. It is raw, unfiltered, and honest. Inside these pages are memories of childhood trauma, abuse, addiction, depression, and suicidal thoughts. Some of what you read may be difficult or triggering.

I am not a counselor, therapist, or doctor. I am a survivor. These words are not meant to replace professional help, and they are not written as advice. They are testimony.

If you find yourself in the same kind of darkness I describe here, please don't carry it alone. Reach out. Talk to someone you trust. Call a hotline. Find a counselor or a friend who will listen. You are not weak for needing help. You are human.

If you are in the United States and are in crisis, dial **988** for the Suicide & Crisis Lifeline. If you live outside the U.S., please look up the hotline or emergency number available in your country.

Take care of yourself as you read. Step away if you need to. Come back only when you are ready. Your story matters, too.

Dedication

First, I dedicate this book to God, the One who carried me when I wanted to give up, turned my cries into testimony, and reminded me that my life had purpose even in darkness. Without His grace, neither these words nor I would exist.

To my mom, I honor your strength in facing your battles and rebuilding your life. You showed me that change is possible, no story is too broken, and love can return after the storm.

To my aunt, for every time you stood in the gap, for every sacrifice, and for always showing up. You were my safe place, steady hand, and reminder that family is who stays.

This book is more than my story. It reflects a God who redeems, a mother who grew stronger, and an aunt who never left.

Prologue

The tie dangled from the doorknob, green faded in pale light, frayed at the edges from years of use—staring like a solution I didn't want. I remember entering my room, resolute, with seventeen years of emotional pain and crushed hopes littering the floor. Outside light carved harsh lines on the ceiling; the overhead fan barely stirred the air but agitated everything inside me. My gaze kept returning to the tie, a silent foe against the walls of my mind. I reached for it, then paused. Reached again, my fingers faltering at its meaning. The whole room pressed in, squeezing me.

For seventeen years, grief, shame, and anger weighed heavily on me. Then, at seventeen, I found myself standing at the edge of a precipice. That night, I made a pact with my mother, a solemn promise that we would no longer hide our struggles from each other. Yet it felt more like a farewell to any remaining hope. Years later, the jar finally tipped and the lid popped off, releasing all emotions and secrets we had kept sealed for so long, freeing, yet overwhelming.

I'm from St. Louis. Born and raised in rough neighborhoods where every corner held a story, and half of them reeked of smoke and regret. We moved so often that I learned to shrink myself, always ready to leave, never anchored. I'm the youngest of three, with wide age gaps: five years, then seven. I grew up hearing my siblings' footsteps and feeling the silence they left behind.

I didn't understand much as a kid. The world was whatever adults said it was. Years passed, and in high school, I finally found the language for what had been living inside me: abandonment, shame, survival. Looking back, I realized it began much earlier, my first bruise and the first taste of metal in my mouth, when I was seven.

My father was a ghost whose face would sometimes appear. My mother had different men around; some I liked, some I hated, even before I knew the word. One of them shouted at me but spoke softly to my sister. I saw him crown her and give me scraps. He praised her warmly, then dashed across the room to yell at me, as though I had broken the house. My heart pounded. My shoulders tensed, bracing for his storm of words, trying to absorb each blow.

I learned to tiptoe. Silence became armor. When the storm broke, silence failed—sometimes shattered. He came, bellowing, hurling insults and threats. I sat on the couch, small as a sparrow, absorbing words like punches. I never saw him hit my mother. There were only sounds: her crying behind a closed door, arguments splitting the air, broken sleep, and the knot in my stomach that never loosened.

My aunt worked one job and went to nursing school. For years, she carried her weight and ours, doing what she could to steady us when everything was spinning out of control. My aunt did what saints do—showed up, fought for us in a hundred small ways.

Meanwhile, half the time, my mother was somewhere else. Adults called it 'not home.' I'd only later learn it was rehab.

I clung to friendships like life rafts, searching connections that felt safe and secure. But each bond frayed as quickly as it formed. Sometimes, the wrong ones found me first, offering refuge that was never real. One loss cut deeper than the rest, someone who felt like family but disappeared when I needed them most. Then came the right wrong one: a bottle. A companion that never talked back. It only echoed in the emptiness, filling the void with its hollow promise of solace.

There was a man—my brother and sister's father—who showed up and felt like belonging. I clutched his old driver's license as proof that my life had meaning. I told people, loud and proud, "That's my daddy." When he smiled at me, I felt real. More than once, he made promises I carried like scripture: that he would always be there, that I could count on him, that he would never leave me like the others. I held onto those words tight, like a rope keeping me from falling.

But belonging didn't last. By thirteen, chaos at home had turned deadly. One Sunday, my mom drove home from church. He reached over and slit her throat behind the wheel. I wasn't in the car, but I saw the aftermath. The car returned. The metallic scent lingered on the seats; violence hung in the silence. The mess inside seemed unreal, each drop of red a silent scream. I stood there, heart pounding, reaching for a rag to clean what no child should touch. The shock hollowed me out, leaving a silence that pressed on my heart every day after.

I carried the smell, the sight, the silence, and guilt for not being at church, thinking I could've stopped it. That day shattered his promise. Belonging can turn to betrayal in a breath, and some wounds bleed inside for years.

Then, at seven, I learned what "vacation" meant to adults—rehab—when my mother left 'for a while.' Only later did I learn it was rehab. At that age, the truth was only a rumor, clinging to clothes and closed doors. I cried myself to sleep more than I slept. Birthdays, in those years, meant bracing. I waited, eyes shut, for the wreckage of another family party. I slept to survive. Sleep became relief, complete and heavy, as if it were the only thing left.

There are smells from that era—faint traces that still find me. In my later childhood, there were clues I didn't understand then, like the strange use of aluminum foil. Much later, during a health class, a video played, and everything clicked. Knowledge fits together in my mind like an unwelcome puzzle. There had been locked rooms, muffled voices, and gestures that told me—even as a child—that something precious had been lost. I remember the way they avoided my gaze, as if not to disturb a grave.

At eight, I heard my mother scream that she didn't love us. No weary, softened tone—this was a blade, honed and cold. "I don't love you," she spat. She chose something else over us, something I couldn't yet name. At that age, permanency meant nothing. I gripped her words, glass sharp. I held them; they cut.

By thirteen, questions became weapons. 'What's the point?' nested inside, tightening my chest and leaving me numb.

I didn't want to die and be remembered for leaving; I just wanted the noise to stop. I hovered between ending everything and holding on, until exhaustion became its own kind of surrender. In those moments, I wrote my thoughts and let the ink bleed onto paper. My grandmother gave me a small notebook, and I carried it everywhere, filling it with hopeful fragments, stray lines, and pieces of days I wanted to remember. That notebook became my refuge, a way to bring order to my chaos. At night, I cried myself to sleep and withdrew into myself for a while.

If you know that smell or have hidden bruises, sit with me. Even when unnoticed, light finds its way through the smallest openings. Once, I almost hurt myself with a tie, but I chose to sleep instead. I became skilled at pretending, slipping on my armor with a forced laugh or timed joke. "What do you call fake spaghetti? An impasta!" That line often slipped from my lips, my wide smile hiding turmoil. These small performances were my shield, guarding my vulnerability from the world. The story didn't end; it began to unfold. In moments, fueled by unexpected kindness and support, I began to heal. The journey was slow, but hope showed that peace could come from brokenness. I continue my journey with weekly therapy, grounding progress in practice, and sharing the burden with understanding ears. Quietly, the notebook stayed. Its pages capture my story—past scribbles hinting at today's words. A silver thread woven from my past into new strength.

The Flesh Is Heavy

Bodies remember. They keep ledger entries, physical marks, and sensations the mind would rather forget. Mine saved the shocks and silences, the shouted names, and the names never spoken. My flesh kept track of all this, so I didn't have to speak it aloud. One memory stands out: a sharp sting on my forearm. The texture of the raised scar felt smooth yet foreign against my skin. It was as if my body was logging an entry I hoped to forget. Each touch imprinted it deeper, the memory louder than words.

The first burden I carried wasn't my own. It was a promise. My brother and sister's father once looked down at me and vowed he'd always be there. He said I could rely on him. I gripped those words like a lifeline thrown to me in chaos. When our house trembled or my mother's muffled crying crept under doors, I held onto that promise. It was the rope I clung to when everything else felt unstable.

Promises break.

Sunday started as usual. My mother drove to church; I stayed home. Hours slipped by, both meaningful and hollow. Then her car returned, carrying a silence thick as a stain. Someone told me, in bits and pieces, what happened. On the drive home, he reached across and used a knife against her. The word 'knife' dropped like a stone. My heart rattled in response, each beat mirroring the shock of that truth. My breath snagged; air turned sharp, cutting through the quiet around me. I did not witness it—only heard about the violence in that car. The immediate aftermath was her absence, a void where her safety and presence should have been. She survived, but everything shifted. The aftermath clung to the silence, in the choppy retellings, I gathered to understand the senseless act.

They brought the car into the driveway. I remember being handed a rag and told to wipe, to clean, to try making a shattered space feel normal again. The car door opened, and the smell hit me first— strong and clinging, it seemed impossible to wash from my clothes or memory. Then I saw the seat, streaked and dark, where no child should have to look. My hands moved because they had to, erasing stains as my mind raced back to the promise—my rope, and the unbearable snap when it broke.

Guilt took root like a thorny seed. I scrubbed the seats with fury. Muscles strained, raw knuckles throbbing as if to erase more than grime. The rag snagged stubbornly, like a memory engraved in my skin—harsh and unyielding. My shoulders ached with exertion, mirroring the 'what ifs' gnawing at my heart. The motion was endless, pain I could not voice pressing in. Each swipe became a wordless plea: maybe, with enough effort, I could undo what had settled in. If I'd gone to church that morning—if I had been there—maybe it wouldn't have happened. Maybe the promise would have kept, sheltering her. Maybe she would have been safe. That irrational blame fused to me, rooted as tenaciously as the stains marring more than fabric; they marked me.

As an adult, I realize the futility of that self-imposed guilt. I've come to understand that the actions of others are beyond my control, that I was not responsible for the violence that unfolded. Yet, that guilt shaped me, teaching me compassion and resilience. It's a reminder of the innocence of childhood, when we believe we have power over the things we do not. I've learned to forgive myself for holding onto that blame and to let it inform my understanding of others who carry similar weight. What would I tell that child now? Perhaps I would ask: If you could see now what burdened your heart then, would you find the courage to lay it down? This reflection invites us all to consider our own past and ask ourselves what burdens we are ready to release.

The flesh is heavy because it remembers more than facts. It stores memories of your own hands repeating actions not meant for you. It echoes the rupture when a vow breaks—the moment the rope you cling to slips away, and the shock of realizing someone trusted can become suddenly dangerous.

School became performance. I practiced smiling until it felt natural. I laughed with classmates as lockers clanged around us. There was a moment—an unguarded second—when my smile slipped. It exposed a flicker of the truth beneath. My chest constricted, shrinking smaller. I learned to answer "I'm fine" without coughing. I mastered invisibility: present, unnoticed.

Yet the body always tells the truth. Beneath my skin dwelled old remnants: the rag in my hand, the lingering odor, the broken promise. They waited, dense, until I learned to shoulder them without breaking. Over time, I learned to lighten the load. The kindness of friends, the flow of time, and writing offered solace. These became bridges to healing, letting me turn heaviness into stories with their own glow. The brightest moment arrived: when pen met paper. Each stroke spun threads of hope into every word, brightening the shadows of my past.

When adults fall apart, you make yourself smaller. You think that's how you survive. But survival leaves marks. Flesh remembers. It keeps the mark. Sometimes that mark becomes the way you tell your story.

Silence Screams

The night before my birthday, the world broke inside my chest.

It started small. An anger sharp and metallic. It swelled, pressing outward, until even the walls seemed to listen. Voices rose—tangled like shards.

A laugh twisted into a snarl.

A question turned into a demand.

Doors slammed hard, rattling the pictures.

There was a rhythm to it: shout, stomp, slam, repeat. I learned the pattern by heart.

I stayed beneath the covers. The covers were a country with borders I could control. Under there, the house faded into a distant blur, except for the storm's rawest shouts. Each syllable from the fight thudded through the mattress—my name, sharp accusations, promises cracking open. My breath was a tiny anchor against the trembling cotton. Outside, the city forced its sleep. Inside, everything pulsed awake and furious. It demanded to be seen.

I remember the taste of that night—metallic at the back of my throat, like pennies held and spat out. I remember the heat from the hall. I remember the smell of someone who'd smoked too long, and another carrying a chemical stench. The television flickered in the other room, a blue ghost while the real drama played out. I counted the seconds between each slam, keeping score as if it were a sport I'd lose if I fell asleep.

Sometimes I thought if I stayed still enough, the noise would pass around me instead of through me. I pressed my face into the pillow until the fibers were imprinted into my cheek. The pillow smelled like powder and the faint perfume of a night out — a memory of a face I hadn't seen in months. My hands clenched the sheet at my sides. I put my thumb in my mouth like a child because being small felt safer than being seen.

The shouting was a knife. It cut clean, then waited, humming to see what would bleed. Words made the house tilt: accusations I'd carry for years, promises I'd later recognize as excuses. Doors slammed. Someone left and returned, leaving a silence that crept in like fog— thick, cold, unreadable. I heard a raw cry, not for show. It slipped into the spaces between furniture, lodging there. Then the yelling drilled—low, destructive. The house felt hollow.

When the sky began to bruise toward morning, I forced my eyes closed even harder. Birthdays are supposed to have candles, songs, and small paper hats that fold at the edges. They are supposed to have cake and a voice that says, 'Happy birthday, baby.' I wanted those things in the way a thirsty man wants water. But overnight, the house had been reshaped into something that couldn't hold a party. My birthday didn't stand a chance against the architecture of rage. This experience shaped my feelings about celebrations for years to come. Whenever my birthday approached, it reminded me of a wish unfulfilled, a day that once symbolized joy but had turned into an echo of silent battles. For a long time, I struggled to see the joy in any celebration, always expecting the shadow of past disappointments to redefine it. Yet, gradually, the longing for brighter birthdays became a whisper of hope rather than a cry of despair, teaching me to create my own quiet moments of happiness even in the simplest of celebrations.

I lay there and asked myself the things a child asks when his world tilts: Who will make my day feel normal? Who will walk into the kitchen and pretend everything's fine? The answer was the same one I had been practicing since I was little: nobody would. We didn't get normal visits. We have words that leave bruises and exits that leave holes.

I remember thinking, in that fetal hush just before dawn, that maybe if I didn't come out of bed, the house would think I was still asleep and be gentle. Maybe if I stayed small and quiet, the adults would forget to rip the rest of the day apart. I counted backward from a hundred, and when I reached thirty, I started again. Time became a shield. Sleep became a trick.

When my mother or one of them knocked on my door that morning — or when the heavy steps announced themselves outside like a judge at the door — I pretended to sleep so long it became an act of will. My stomach churned with a sickness that had nothing to do with food. The smell of last night's arguments still clung to the air, like someone had burned something and left the smoke to hang on the curtains.

Eventually, I rose because the world demands movement—even when you are broken. I tiptoed out as I had done a thousand times before. Palms sticky with the remains of some long-ago snack. My brother and sister were somewhere ahead of me in the day's script. They navigated the silence with a practiced ease, each in their own way. My brother, always the peacemaker, would try to defuse the tension with jokes, his laughter echoing through the halls in strained attempts to fill the void; my sister, on the other hand, wore her resilience like armor, her eyes distant as if she saw a world beyond these walls. Next, I practiced their calm like a costume. Steeling myself, I walked into the living room, expecting the ruins of last night: empty bottles on the counter, a cushion thrown across the floor, the coffee pot cold. What I found was worse and quieter—a careful silence that had the shape of a pardon withheld.

There was no candle, no song, no paper hat. There was a plate half-full of scrambled eggs and a long apology that none of us could afford. Later, someone would say, "We'll celebrate tonight," and somewhere inside me another small thing folded and died a little. The promise of celebration is a sting if the wounded are still raw. I learned that day that postponement can be a form of harm.

School that day was a theater. I rehearsed normally. I sat in class with a manufactured smile; more fragile than the paper hats they put on babies. The other kids asked if I'd had a good time, and I said, "Yeah." As if the three letters could repair a house. The lie fits into my mouth like a habit. No one asked what the night sounded like. No one had to. They were living their own loud lives; my silence was an uninvited extra.

The memory of that birthday changed me. As the emptiness of the morning settled, it gave me perspective, forcing me to reflect on the aftermath of silence. It taught me that absence adds up, quiet mornings stacking until silence feels inevitable. It showed me how to fold pain into the day and wear the lack of celebration like a coat. It revealed that joy can be rationed or stolen, and promises exist to tide you over until ruin recedes. Yet in that stillness, I also detected the faintest echo of resilience, a suggestion that silence, once understood, could shape not just sorrow but also strength. This whisper of future healing hinted that, despite everything, there might come a time when I could forge a new kind of quiet, one that harbored not only the echoes of the past but seeds for a gentler dawn.

But the cruelest lesson was also the seed of something else: I learned that I could survive a day without a party. I learned that my throat could choke down a lie and keep functioning. I learned that I could move through the world like a ghost and still come back to myself. It was a small thing, but a thing nonetheless — survival as habit.

Later, when the nights didn't end in yelling and the candles came, sometimes lit by people who meant it, I would learn how to receive them. I would learn to distinguish between a promise made to postpone and a promise kept. For now, on that birthday, I learned how to be small and how to hide the way silence screams.

After that birthday, I realized I had lied so much that I couldn't remember the first time I lied about being fine. "Fine" became my second name. It was stitched across my chest like a label I couldn't take off. At school, in the neighborhood, even at home when the walls still hummed from last night's yelling, I wore "Fine" like armor. Beneath this armor, constant buzzing was audible. A low-grade hum of static was always in the background. My chest felt tight, as though my ribs were holding in the words I couldn't say. Nobody questioned armor. Nobody wanted to see the skin underneath anyway. Teachers noted my quiet demeanor but never pressed further. Friends were dazzled by the facade of normalcy I maintained. It was like living in a theater where the show never stopped. No one peered beyond the curtain.

"Fine" was easier than telling the truth. Easier than saying my birthday smelled like cigarettes and old beer cans. Easier than explaining why I flinched when the door slammed or why my body shook when somebody laughed too loudly. "Fine" kept me from having to unpack the mess in front of people who weren't ready to hear it. Even the occasional concerned glance from a kind teacher. A knowing look from the neighbor went unnoticed or unspoken.

But "Fine" was stolen from me. It trapped my real self deep inside. Each time I said it, another piece hid beneath the floorboards, away from the chance to be seen. Fine" grew heavier every day, spreading darkness over my light. It was false comfort, a cloak I couldn't cast off, even as I whispered it to myself and disappeared further.

The truth was never fine. The truth was:

> I was terrified of silence because I knew it always meant something hurtful was coming next.

> I hated birthdays because everyone made me feel invisible and unwanted.

> I tasted alcohol before I tasted love.

I carried shame heavier than any bookbag I slung across my shoulders.

But you don't say those things at thirteen. You don't say them when your peers are bragging about sneakers and girls. You don't say them when teachers are asking for homework you couldn't focus on. You don't say them when your mom is locked in a room with her demons, and you're too young to name them. You just smile, laugh at the right time, and keep saying "I'm fine."

"Fine" became my religion. My daily prayer. My cover story. And soon, I believed it. I tricked myself just as I had tricked everyone else. If I could convince the world, maybe I could convince my heart that I wasn't breaking.

But silence screams. Eventually, the body leaks what the mouth refuses to say. My silence emerged in clenched fists, in doors I slammed myself, and in eyes that lingered on ceiling fans for too long. It seeped into the burn of liquor and the sting of lies that tasted sweet going down, but poisoned me slowly. As an adult, I've come to recognize how these childhood patterns, woven into me, have shaped my responses and relationships. While I've learned to find my voice and speak my truth, the echoes of those silent screams still teach me about the resilience and strength I've carried with me into the present day.

"Fine"

Fine is a mask with teeth.

It smiles wide and swallows whole.

It claps at parties, nods in classrooms,

and sits at the dinner table like a guest

who never leaves.

But when the lights go out,

Fine rips itself open

and screams in the dark.

Addictions, Distractions, and the Empty Fix

Winter break was meant to be joy: crunching footsteps on snow, the scent of pine, kids' laughter outside, and the cozy glow of Christmas lights. For me, though, it was just the quiet hum of the heater trying to fill the heavy silence. No school, no friends—only the house, the silence, and me beneath everything I wished to forget. Loneliness replaced laughter. The cheerful facade around me only deepened the ache, a reminder of what was missing. I longed for connection, for a sign I existed beyond the quiet.

That's when I found my first friend. What followed was not a person or a hand to hold, but a bottle, something always within reach when everything else felt far away.

It started small, but its impact quickly grew. The first time I held alcohol, I was eight.

A can of beer: warm, bitter, nasty. Heavier than I expected, not meant for me. The room smelled oddly sharp and sweet. I swallowed anyway because the men laughed at me and called me "grown." They saw a punchline, not a child. I hated the taste but loved the attention. Maybe this was what growing up meant, a way in.

By twelve, it wasn't a joke anymore. In my hand: a full bottle of champagne—cold, fizzing, alive. I tilted it back and swallowed. For the first time in my life, I felt something close to peace. The sweetness rushed through me and sparked in my chest. Edges of pain numbed, unwanted feelings blurring. No longer was I the kid hiding under covers on his birthday, trying to block out the echo of my parents arguing in the next room. Nor was I the boy who heard his mother screaming that she didn't love him. I was somebody. This, I realized, was the best thing I'd ever tasted.

By thirteen, I graduated. I sat at the table, playing spades with my brother and my sister's father. The cards slapped against the wood, and music hummed low in the background. Our voices rose and fell as the game unfolded, each bid and banter adding to the rhythm that tied us together. When my sister's father slid a glass across to me—not beer, not bubbles, but hard liquor—the burn traced a line from my throat to my stomach, fire spreading through my ribs. We laughed and shared stories, the camaraderie as intoxicating as the drink. I drank again. This time, I didn't hate the burn; I welcomed it. The burn felt like it was burning something out of me.

That winter, alcohol became my hiding place. When the house screamed, the bottle whispered. Silence pressed down, but the bottle lifted me up. My birthday felt empty; with alcohol, I felt full. This pattern sets the tone for years to follow.

But here's the lie: alcohol never heals. At first, the numbing relief disguised itself as comfort, masking pain with a sense of emptiness. I didn't realize at thirteen that the fleeting sense of belonging and relief was hollow. For a while, alcohol made me feel accompanied during the winter, offering a surface escape from the loneliness that filled the house. Beneath that escape, however, the ache remained—hidden but unresolved, making the emptiness more profound each time the temporary comfort faded. I thought I had discovered a friend, a way to make it through the cold, but underneath, I was losing myself.

Reflecting on these memories now, I recognize my belief in alcohol's comfort as deeply misguided. The shift from thinking alcohol helped me to understand it was an impostor is stark: True healing, I've since learned, does not arrive suddenly but grows from facing and feeling the very pain I once tried to escape. The vulnerability I once avoided has become a source of strength, and the connection I once sought in a bottle is found, in truth, only by risking being seen and known by others. Every step toward healing required me to leave behind the false sense of safety that addiction offered and to risk reaching out to others instead.

Really, I was learning to disappear. But deep inside, a quiet voice questioned if there was more, if I could ever truly be seen. In rare moments, I wondered about claiming a place in warmth that always seemed just out of reach. That faint wish later guided me to seek healing and connection, steering me toward transformation.

"First Friend"

The can was bitter.

The bottle was sweet.

The glass was fire.

Each one promised comfort,

each one kept me warm,

each one took a piece of me

I didn't know I'd miss.

When Flesh Fails

The body can only carry so much before it begins to leak. Mine had been leaking for years. Through clenched jaws.

Through fake smiles.

Through bottles drained too young.

But the flood came later.

Seventeen years of pain left no more places to retreat. Every 'I'm fine' built an invisible wall inside my chest, heavy as bricks weighing me down. Each slammed door, every night spent crying myself to sleep, every birthday I pretended didn't matter—these memories pressed in, waiting their turn. When the waiting ended, my body gave up, unable to hold back the flood any longer.

It wasn't dramatic, not like fireworks or screaming. Instead, it was me, alone in my room, staring at a tie draped over the doorknob and the ceiling fan spinning above me. The air felt thick and oppressive. The musty warmth of the room clung to my skin, a reminder that life persisted. My chest tightened with each shallow breath, as though the tie and the fan—so ordinary on any other night—became the symbols of a decision, each holding the weight of my life in balance: a strip of cloth versus a spinning blade.

I went back and forth. Tie, fan. Fan, tie. My body shook. My mind raced. My chest felt like it was caving in; seventeen years of silence screamed at once. I couldn't quiet it. My flesh said, *Enough.*

I wanted the noise to be gone. I wanted the taste of fear, the echo of insults burned away. The memory of fists and the chemical sting of lost birthdays haunted me, and I longed for those ghosts to fall silent. Even the silence itself, the one that screamed the loudest, became unbearable.

I reached. My hand brushed the tie. My eyes lifted to the fan. Tears blurred everything. I thought of being eight, hearing my mother say she didn't love me. I thought of being twelve, clutching a bottle like it was salvation. I thought of being thirteen, burning liquor down my throat while men laughed. I thought of every time I lied, "I'm fine," until I couldn't remember the first lie anymore.

And then I cried myself to sleep. I didn't die. Not that night. But something inside me broke open and spilled everywhere. Flesh failed, but somehow, spirit refused. When I woke the next morning, the room was unfamiliar, as if the world had shifted while I slept. My mind was foggy, and my body felt heavy, weighed down by the turmoil of the previous night. There was a distinct sense of emptiness, an absence of the usual noise that had filled my head, replaced instead by a hum of cautious quiet. I lay there for a moment, feeling the rough imprint of the pillow against my cheek, aware of how close I had come to an ending. My heart beat slower, the realization settling slowly that I was still here, still breathing. Though nothing outside had changed, internally, a different landscape began to take shape—one where survival, for the first time, felt like an active decision rather than a resigned conclusion.

The thing about breaking points is this: sometimes they don't end you. Sometimes they expose you. Sometimes they force you to see that survival and living are not the same thing. That night taught me a single, undeniable truth: surviving is merely existing, while living is daring to embrace life beyond the shadows.

There's a slow way to die and a fast way to break. I'd lived long with the slow way—the quiet erosion from old wounds opening and closing until scar tissue forgot softness. But breaking is quick. It hits like bad weather: the sky looks unchanged until the first thunder, then everything rushes forward.

They told me to pack that night, as if we were leaving for good. Not the usual "vacation" lie; this was colder, a clipped sentence with no heart behind it. There was an agreement between me and my mother that sat in the air like a verdict. I don't remember each syllable, only the way the sentence landed: final. It was more of an instruction than a conversation. Maybe she wanted me to go somewhere else. Maybe she meant it as punishment. Maybe she was tired of being careful around the edges of our lives. Whatever it was, the result felt like being folded into a paper bag and set aside.

When you've been small inside a house that argues, the body learns to inventory itself. I counted scars like currency and memories like debts. The agreement was the last straw because it felt like confirmation—a punctuation mark on seventeen years of being unchosen. All those nights pretending the shouting meant nothing, all the mornings swallowing 'fine' like a pill, all the times I hid behind laughter so adults wouldn't see the hollow inside—it all added up, and the math came to one painful solution: I was alone. Yet, as I recounted these wounds, a small part of me recognized that this accounting was not only a tally of pain but the starting point of reclaiming my narrative. In acknowledging the scars, I inadvertently began rejecting the idea of accumulating more. I realized that, by confronting my past, I was taking the first step toward refusing to let it continue to define me.

You would think an ending would be literal — a scream, a fight, someone catching you. It wasn't. The most dangerous things are ordinary: a tie hung on a hook, a ceiling fan that had been spinning since before dawn. Two common things became the vocabulary of a decision.

I remember the room in intimate, petty detail. The poster on the wall was slouching because the tape had lost its stick. A sliver of streetlight cut across the floor in the shape of a rectangle. My sneaker lay by the bed, one sock inside and one out, like a child who'd been interrupted mid-dress. My pillow had an imprint of the place I'd pressed my face so many nights. At one end of the room, the doorknob had a tie looped through it — a rope of possibility. Above, the ceiling fan moved like a slow metronome, patient as anything that waits to be put to use.

I paced because pacing kept me from listening to the small, precise thoughts. Each step was a stave in a song that said, You *are not enough; you are expendable; you will not be missed.* My hand found the tie like a moth finds light. It was a simple fabric, inexpensive, and the color had already faded. I wrapped it around my fingers until the texture stopped being texture and became a script — letters I could read if I wanted to: enough, finished, over.

I thought about ending it because ending promised an answer. It promised silence that wasn't angry. It promised rest that didn't come from sleep. Yet, amidst the hopelessness, a faint whisper of remembrance occasionally broke through, offering a fleeting pause. The thoughts were not a single moment of madness; they were the final tally of years of being told with words and actions that I was less. Each memory stacked on top of the other until the idea made sense. Why continue when the world has not bothered to choose you all these years?

But memory is also stubborn in the other direction. It throws you a rope when you are most practiced in letting go. I thought of my aunt in nursing school, and the familiar scent of oil and rubber greeted me every time I watched her work in the dim light of the living room. Despite her long shifts, she always found the energy to fix the flat tire on my bike, making sure I could ride again. I thought of my teacher who said, "Hey, you okay?" and actually waited for the answer without looking away, his pen clicking gently as he leaned back in his chair, creating a rhythm that seemed to assure me that time was ours, just for a moment.

These were small things, moments that felt too minor to matter, but in that hour, they were lighthouse beams cutting through the fog. They didn't erase the storm, but they reminded me I wasn't completely lost in it.

I went back and forth between the hand and the ceiling fan like a pendulum between two options. The room narrowed to three things: the tie, the fan, and the space between my next breath. I tested the air like a diver finding the surface. Nothing in the room convinced me to stay; nothing screamed at me to go. So, I did the only thing I'd practiced for years with hurting: I cried-slept.

Crying to sleep is not a form of peace. It is surrender. The body flattens—too tired to keep arguing with itself. When sleep took me, it wasn't soft and comforting but heavy, bone-deep exhaustion. Tear tracks dried into salt lines I later traced with my fingertips, reading braille.

I woke up the next morning like someone caught mid-sentence and put in parentheses. Nothing had changed. The tie hung the same. The fan hummed on, its relentless spinning a stark contrast to my heartbeat, which now stuttered in a new, uneasy tempo. The house continued as if nothing had touched it the night before. That ordinary continuity is one of the cruelest things about breaking: the world keeps its rhythm, and you are left rearranging the pieces that used to be you.

But that morning, I also realized something else: failure of the flesh does not require death to change you. The act of coming back from that edge rewired the room. It made the bed into a witness and the pillow into a diary. The tie became a marker of a night I survived. It shifted the grammar of my life from the quiet acceptance of being unchosen to a question: What *now?* The fan kept spinning, but the spinning no longer felt like a threat; it felt like a timer that I had paused.

In those early days, I took small but significant steps towards seeking help and healing. I reached out to a friend who'd once said they cared, breaking the silence I'd maintained for years. I searched for local support groups, places where I could share and listen without judgment. I began journaling daily, a process that slowly turned my confusion into clarity. Each entry was a small release, a step toward understanding my own story. Eventually, I sought professional help, making an appointment with a counselor who guided me through the tangled web of my past. Meeting with them provided me with an anchor, reminding me that asking for help was not a sign of weakness but a brave step toward reclaiming my narrative.

Breaking opened me up in a way quiet endurance never could. It forced me to bring the secret into the light, at least to myself. The body failed, but the spirit, stubbornly, infuriatingly, held on. That refusal to finish the sentence birthed the first shameful courage I ever had: the courage to be honest with myself, to admit I needed help, and to begin, haltingly, to ask for it.

As the days unfolded, I discovered something unexpected: the healing tools I once ignored became avenues to honor this stubborn spirit. I began to journal, my pen moving like a steady hand tracing the lines of my past, shedding the weight of silence. Breathing deeply, I turned inward, learning to quiet the internal storm and find peace. Bit by bit, I let movement guide me, from the rhythm of tapping feet to the meditative embrace of yoga. These practices, though small, transformed the refusal to end into a blossoming action that paved the road for healing and growth.

"Not Finished"

The tie was ordinary.

The fan was ordinary.

My choice could have been ordinary, too.

But flesh failed, and the rest did not.

I reached the end and found only the next morning,

raw and terrible and mine.

I breathed.

And breathing was the smallest rebellion.

The Cry No One Hears

There is a quiet pain for those who hide their feelings. It's not a shout, nor a sob anyone can hear. Instead, it's a steady ache in the chest, like waiting for night. I called it the cry no one hears. Most nights, I whispered it to myself, pretending the whisper would soothe me. I remember the weight of my blanket and the way moonlight made shapes on my wall. In those moments, the stillness made the ache feel as real as my heartbeat.

After the night with the tie and the fan, the thought did not go away. It stayed with me, almost like a quiet visitor standing nearby, always present.

Sometimes it felt like a heavy fog that made mornings dull and afternoons slow. Other times, it became a clear thought: What's the point? That thought sat with me like an unnoticed guest, and I learned to ignore it like so many other things.

But the morning after, something changed. I woke up and, with a small amount of courage, I went to school. I walked into the counselor's office with the posters and soft chairs. I said the words I had held for years. I told her everything I could: the knot of fear, the memory of the tie and fan, and the long tally of being unchosen. Saying *I need help* felt like dropping a stone into a lake. The ripples started small and then spread. Not everyone has a counselor or safe adult. Sometimes it feels like there is no one to listen without judgment. If this is your reality, consider reaching out to helplines, trusted friends, or teachers. Sometimes a small connection can show you're not alone in your silence.

The counselor did not laugh. She did not tell me to "get over it." She listened. Then she did the thing adults sometimes do right: she reached out. My mother and my aunt were called to the school. When they arrived, the room that had been private turned ordinary and sharp at once. Faces I loved sat across from me, and I felt both seen and exposed. They decided to take me to the hospital.

The hospital was not a punishment. It felt like both an ending and a beginning. I stayed there for four days. Four days that altered the way the rest of my life would be read. The first day was dense with forms and questions, as well as the small rituals of being examined. Nurses spoke in voices that tried to be neutral but were softer than the ones I'd grown used to hearing at home. A doctor asked me to tell the story again — the one I had already told — and listened in a way I had not expected.

Those four days were filled with slow, careful attention that was new and needed. Someone gave me a clean-smelling blanket. Someone showed me how to breathe to calm panic. There were visits and quiet times. I learned that a room could hold someone falling apart without judging them. Those days helped me learn to name my feelings, practice asking for help, and understand that a crisis can be a chance for change, not an end to life.

Being in the hospital didn't fix everything or erase every memory. But it did something crucial: it broke the secrecy for a moment. My cry was finally heard by more than ghosts. My aunt and my mother, both wrestling with their own struggles, could see what they had missed. The hospital allowed me to develop a plan with others, including counselors and therapists, and provided regular check-ins. I began regular therapy, set up self-care routines, and scheduled weekly check-ins with trusted friends or family. These steps didn't fix things right away, but they started my path to recovery and gave me ways to manage emotions once left unspoken.

People often think suicidal thoughts come suddenly, like lightning. For me, it was more like a slow tide. It gathered in the corners of each day and lingered in conversation, even when ignored. I learned to hide it. I joked at the right moments, answered texts, and built one false front after another until it looked like life.

The cry no one hears is hard to recognize because it doesn't always make you want to act. Sometimes, it just numbs you, quieting the world so nothing hurts. It can feel like a tempting offer: take away one pain and, make tomorrow easier. And when you grow up thinking your life matters less, these offers feel logical and true.

The loneliness of those thoughts is not just being alone. It also means lacking purpose. It's feeling that your words won't change anything, that sharing will be ignored, judged, or used against you. When your mother said she didn't love you, believing someone could bear that and not break felt impossible. Who wants to cause trouble and make others face unwelcome problems? Still, remember: many people fear being judged or dismissed. Yet, some will listen and care, seeing your words as valid. Reaching out can be hard, but someone is there, ready to support and understand.

So you hide your pain deep inside. You ignore it and pretend it doesn't matter—like a letter you keep meaning to open. Each day, you put it off, and eventually, ignoring it becomes routine.

Sometimes the cry reminded me of the past: nights when I was scared by slamming doors, drinking champagne to feel safe, being told to act grown-up too early. It collects memories—people leaving, promises of vacations that never happened, birthdays forgotten—and uses them to convince you that you're not worth much.

Other times, the cry was quiet because it understood shame. There is a special shame reserved for the people who are supposed to be chosen first — children, sons, the ones who are given protection by default. When protection grinds away, there's a hollowness that comes with the realization that you were capable of being unchosen. That shame keeps you silent.

But this cry also raises questions you may not want to answer. Sometimes, in its own way, it makes you ask for help. Maybe that's why memories of kindness—like a neighbor bringing food or a teacher asking if you're okay—can become small lights you follow when you feel lost. Even small kindnesses can guide you when things are dark.

There's no hero moment here. No tidy rescue. For me, the first honest step looked like this: a hand that paused on the tie and then let go; a morning that I decided to stay awake and not finish the sentence; a whispered truth I gave myself in a mirror, ugly and trembling: *I need help.* Saying it wasn't for anyone else at first. It was for me — the boy who had been listening to the cry for years and finally gave it permission to be heard out loud.

Hearing the cry out loud made other feelings possible. It made me start describing exactly where the pain lived: in my chest, in my hands, or in the shake of my voice when I lied. Naming these places is a small first step. Naming isn't therapy itself, but it's a way to begin. When you say, "this hurts here," you make an invisible feeling real. Real things can be examined and understood.

After that night, the real work began — not dramatic, not fast. It was the slow, clumsy work of learning not to let silence be my strategy. It was learning to tell one person, then two. It was learning that there are people who will not run when you speak the thing that the house has kept quiet for you. It was learning that help can look like a phone call, a long, slow sigh of relief when someone listens, or a counselor who does not flinch when you say the worst. I don't want to make recovery sound straightforward. There were relapses: nights when the cry returned louder, months when 'fine' slipped out by habit. But there were small victories, too. One morning, I woke up and did not reach for the bottle. I remember stepping outside. The air was crisp, the sun painted the sky in pastels, and the fresh dew mingled with the aroma of breakfast. This sensory moment—a new day's fragrance—felt like a private victory. There was also a group that held me while I found words for my pain. These moments stacked quietly. One day, I saw that the ledger had more entries of survival than surrender. Over time, the storms grew quieter, days lighter, peace longer. Pain may return, but it does not last for long. Life can brighten as new choices and victories add up. This offers hope to those struggling, showing that healing is a journey toward light.

If you carry the same cry, know this: silence is not the only option. The cry is real, and it deserves to be heard. You deserve people who will not treat your words like gossip or evidence of weakness. There are ways to reach out that do not minimize your pain—they make it shared. Consider texting a helpline where trained listeners can offer support without judgment. Write a note to a trusted friend or family member if speaking feels too daunting. Even a message left on a phone or a simple journal entry beginning to articulate your feelings can invite connection. Initiating a conversation with a teacher or counselor can also be a crucial step forward. These are small acts, but they can open the door to understanding and support.

The morning after the tie and the fan, I did something different: I went to school, walked into my counselor's office, and told the truth. I spilled years of silence in a few trembling sentences. My mom and my aunt were called. When they arrived, their faces held a kind of shock — not anger, not pity, but stunned silence. They didn't know. They never knew. And maybe that was the loudest proof of all: that I had carried this cry so well-hidden, even the people who lived closest to me had no idea.

They decided to take me to the hospital.

The first few hours were spent on paperwork and answering questions, with nurses asking me to repeat what I'd already said. But it was when I looked around that I knew: this wasn't the place for me. The things I saw — kids rocking back and forth in corners, blank stares, some crying out loud with no one rushing fast enough to hold them — showed me pain wears many faces. Pain can be loud, feral, explosive. Mine had been silent. And in that silence, I suddenly realized: if I stayed here, my voice would disappear inside this chaos.

Everyone around me — staff, family, and even classmates who later found out — was shocked. Shocked because I wore "Fine" so well. I was shocked because I had smiled and laughed, and never showed the fracture. Shocked because I had made it this far, hiding from a storm that should've swallowed me whole. Their shock was proof of how deeply I had learned to lie.

I stayed four days. Four days of listening to doors lock behind me, four days of watching strangers cope in ways I didn't recognize, four days of realizing that healing wouldn't come from walls and white coats alone. The hospital was a stop, not a home. It wasn't where I would find myself. But it was a mirror. It showed me that what I carried was real enough to bring me here. It showed the people in my life that I wasn't untouchable, wasn't "fine," wasn't immune. It forced my cry into the open, where denial couldn't cover it anymore.

When I left, I knew I couldn't keep pretending. I couldn't keep calling numbness a survival tactic. I couldn't keep giving silence the microphone. The hospital wasn't my solution, but it was my signal. A line in the sand: I couldn't go back to being invisible in my own story.

Practical Steps (Real, Small, Doable)

1. If you are in immediate danger or thinking about harming yourself, call emergency services or **988** (U.S.) now.

2. Tell one person: pick someone whose hands feel steady — an aunt, an older friend, a coach, anyone. You can say: *"I've been feeling like I might hurt myself. I need help."* The words are heavy but clear.

3. Grounding practice (useful in the moment): name 5 things you can see, 4 things you can touch, 3 things you can hear, 2 things you can smell, and 1 thing you can taste. Repeat until your breathing steadies.

4. Keep a single, private journal entry titled: *Tonight I am safe for now because…* — write one sentence. Add to it nightly. Small entries build a proof-of-survival list.

5. If possible, find a local counselor, pastor, or school social worker who can help make a safety plan. If you don't know one, text or call **988** for immediate support and referrals.

6. If alcohol is part of your coping, consider asking someone to help you remove access temporarily (taking bottles out of the house, agreeing to not drink together). Reach out to

local support groups — you don't have to quit on your own.

"Silent Alarm"

My mouth said nothing,

but my bones were screaming.

I laughed at jokes,

but my chest was on fire.

No one saw the smoke.

No one smelled the burn.

I carried the alarm inside me,

and called it living.

A Crack of Light

The hospital felt like another world. As soon as I arrived, a heavy finality closed in, trapping me in a sterile bubble. The air was sharp, with an antiseptic and faint metallic tang. Lights buzzed overhead with a cold hum, routines clanked—carts on squeaking wheels ticking like a clock. It was a place scrubbed of individuality, where even small comforts vanished under strict rules designed to keep everyone safe.

My family came. They brought me clothes from home because I wasn't allowed to wear what I'd come in. I remember the bag, the faces, the way the air smelled different when someone tried to bring ordinary things into a place where ordinary wasn't allowed. They had to prepare the clothes before handing them over: the elastic was cut from the waistbands, shoelaces were removed, and pockets were checked and folded neatly. By the time the sweatshirt and sweatpants reached me, they were altered, safe, stripped of anything that could tighten, bind, or be used to do harm. As I pulled the clothes on, the loose waistband brushed against my chilled skin, each touch a reminder of how far away 'normal' felt, how bare and exposed being 'safe' could make you feel.

It should have felt like mercy, but at first, it felt like another kind of taking away. My pants sagged because the waist had been altered.

My shoes sat awkwardly without laces. My aunt tried to laugh it off when she handed them to me, to make the moment small and normal, but the change sat on my skin like a quiet accusation: I was someone who needed to be watched, controlled, kept from myself. Yet, even as I stood there, wrapped in altered clothes, I could feel a flicker of resolve within me. I wasn't just a passive recipient of these changes. I was still myself, defiant under the weight of what I needed to wear. In that realization, a glimmer of strength emerged. I could still craft my own narrative, even here, learning to find control in small, subtle ways, sensing that this might be the start of something new.

Still, there was something in the fact that they came. In the way my aunt stood there, exhausted from work, holding a bag of clothes she had made ready so I could have something that smelled like home. In the way my mom looked at me — not angry, not performative, but stunned and raw, like she'd just discovered the depth of what I'd been carrying. Their presence didn't fix the night the car came home or erase the promise that had snapped. It didn't erase the rag in my hand or the smell that wouldn't leave. But it meant I mattered enough to bother with.

The days inside were long. Group therapy felt like being in a room of static and mismatched voices. I hated the place; it made me feel small. Watching the other kids' silence, which was sometimes explosive, showed me what could happen if I continued to hide. They weren't miracles; they were warnings and company at once. I recall a girl named Sarah, who sat across from me nearly every day. Her eyes always moved, never settling long, as if searching for something lost. One afternoon during a break, she sat beside me and whispered, "Do you ever feel like you're just... stuck in a loop?" Her words hung between us, heavy with understanding. I nodded, feeling the weight of her question. "Every single day," I replied. For that moment, we weren't alone in our isolation—both searching for a way out. It was quiet solidarity, a struggle in her shifting eyes and my own.

A nurse taught me a breathing exercise called the 4-7-8 technique. I inhaled for four counts, held my breath for seven, then exhaled for eight. A counselor asked me, 'What are you hoping for tomorrow?' and listened closely. They couldn't promise much, but they gave me the tools and calm words I needed.

The hospital didn't save me. It didn't cure the nights or clear the stains from memory. But it gave me a pause, like standing at a cliff edge in moonlight—my rush to the edge interrupted. In that stillness, even the altered sweatpants mattered. They reminded me that somebody noticed I was falling and tried, awkwardly and tenderly, to help.

After I was discharged, I stepped into the world with cautious renewal. The hospital pause allowed me to breathe, and with the tools they provided, I saw light through the leaves of my journey. On crisp mornings, the warm breath of life in the cold air showed the world's lingering brightness. The journey was slow. Setbacks and shadows returned, but now I noticed a faint trail away from the edge. Gradually, I learned to find my path, holding onto the hope that had begun in the hospital, as if the transition itself had opened a new door.

"First Light"

It wasn't a sunrise.

It wasn't a miracle.

It was a crack

thin as a thread,

barely there.

But through it,

I saw a world

where I wasn't finished.

And that was enough

to keep breathing.

Learning to Breathe Again

The room was quiet except for the monitors beeping and nurses moving softly. I lay there, the hospital gown cold against my skin, as I took my first shaky inhale. It wasn't the victorious gasp after surfacing underwater, but a fragile breath, each inhale threatening to break. Doubts and uncertainty pressed in, making healing seem impossible. But that's okay. It's normal to feel fragile and unsure, to question the process. Healing didn't strike like lightning. There was no miraculous moment when pain vanished. It began with something smaller: learning how to breathe again.

At the hospital, a nurse showed me a trick. "Put your hand on your chest," she said. "Take a slow breath, feel it rise. Hold, then release." I looked at her, skeptical. *Did she think breathing solved anything?* I needed solutions, not this. She made me practice as if it were homework. "It feels stupid," I muttered, half-hoping she wouldn't hear. She smiled gently. "Trust me. Sometimes, the simplest things help most." At first, it felt pointless. But when panic pressed down, that simple breath was all I had. Along with breathing, she suggested touching something textured or counting sounds, like footsteps or beeps. These small grounding techniques became anchors when the world felt overwhelming.

So, I kept at it. Continuing what the nurse showed me; breathing became my first act of rebellion. My life had been a blur of distractions, a frantic chase to drown out the chaos. Breathing was the opposite: still, deliberate, mine. Each breath was a protest against the thoughts that told me I didn't belong here. Each exhale was proof I was still alive.

But breathing wasn't just about oxygen. It was about slowing down enough to truly feel. For years, I had avoided feelings, drowned them in bottles, smothered them under 'I'm fine,' and buried them in silence. Breathing forced me to sit in my body, to actually notice the tension in my jaw, the ache in my chest, the tremor in my hands, the memories hiding behind my ribs. There was a tightness in my throat and a tingling in my palms, each sensation an echo of the trauma that lurked within. It was terrifying, but these physical cues were also the first step toward not running from myself. It's essential to acknowledge that these challenging emotions are a natural part of the healing process. Feeling discomfort or fear doesn't mean failure; it simply means you're progressing, however slowly. It's okay to take things at your own pace, allowing your journey to unfold gently over time.

Learning to breathe again meant learning new rhythms:

Waking up and telling myself, *just make it through the next hour,* instead of the whole day.

Writing down one sentence in a notebook: *I'm still here.*

Sitting outside for five minutes, letting cold air bite my face, reminding myself that the world was bigger than my pain.

It wasn't glamorous. No applause, no parades for surviving another morning. Every intentional breath was a quiet victory. Each breath meant choosing life, even when I wasn't sure why. In those moments, I learned to pause, listen to the gentle voice within that whispered, "You're doing well, keep going." This inner kindness reaffirmed that breathing wasn't merely a matter of survival; it was an act of self-care and compassion.

I stumbled, of course. There were nights when I reached for the bottle instead of my breath. Nights when I let anger or numbness win. But the difference now was that I knew another way existed. I had a tool. I had proof that even in the middle of panic, I could anchor myself back with something as small as air. Setbacks happened, but they didn't erase the progress I had made. Instead, they became reminders to practice self-forgiveness and acknowledge that recovery isn't a straight line. They taught me resilience, illustrating that each fall was just another opportunity to rise again, stronger and with a deeper understanding of my journey.

Breath became prayer. Breath became anchor. Breath became a promise: no matter what else fails, I will keep breathing. With each breath, I reclaimed a piece of myself. That is how healing began, the quiet rebellion of staying alive. Yet, beyond mere survival, a possibility glimmered: the thought of sharing my story, perhaps to help someone else find their breath, lit a small spark of purpose within me. It whispered that maybe, just maybe, this journey could lead to something more, a life not just endured, but fully embraced.

I invite you, dear reader, to pause and think about your own small victories. Perhaps you, too, have moments that, while seemingly insignificant, have meant the world to you. Sharing those stories, whether with loved ones or simply with yourself, creates meaningful connections. By reflecting on our personal triumphs, we foster a community of shared hope and resilience. Let us remember that every breath and every step taken contributes to our collective healing.

"Breath"

Inhale — the weight sits heavy.

Exhale — it loosens a little.

Inhale — the memories claw.

Exhale — they release, not all at once, but enough.

Every breath is a bargain.

Every breath is a seed.

I am alive.

And that is enough for now.

The Mirror and the Scar

There's a moment after the tears have dried and your chest stops heaving with fear. After endless hours in a hospital bed, the sharp scent of antiseptic hangs in the air. The distant echo of footsteps down the hallway is the only sound breaking the silence. In that moment, you finally stand still long enough to really see yourself. Not the mask that fools others. Not the forced 'I'm fine.' Just you: exposed, trembling, heart pounding, absolutely real.

For me, it was the mirror.

At first, I hated what I saw. It was the face I didn't want, eyes heavy beyond my years. My shoulders were burdened by weights no child should carry. My body was hypersensitive to every sound, remembering each slammed door and shout that pierced the night.

But the mirror showed more: scars, some hidden, some visible. They mark that something tried to end my life and failed. Shame lingered, suggesting *these scars made me less than whole. Yet these marks weren't silent accusations; they were badges of survival.*

At first, I wanted to erase them. I tried to hide the pain with laughter, clothes, and stories. But the scar remained. And the mirror revealed the truth. I had a choice: keep pretending, or face what the scars meant. My first small step was to spend a few minutes each day in reflection. It wasn't easy. I had to tell myself, "This is your story," and resist turning away. Facing it taught me that healing begins with showing up for yourself, even if just for a moment.

Over time, I saw that scars aren't a weakness. They're records—survival notes written into flesh. When I looked in the mirror and saw the weight under my eyes, it reminded me: I lived through it. When I remembered that night with the tie and the fan, I told myself: *I'm still here.*

Facing the scar meant facing myself. I was the boy who was eight with a beer can in his hand. The twelve-year-old was holding champagne as if it were salvation. The thirteen-year-old was coughing up liquor to earn respect. The teenager lied, "I'm fine," so much so that he forgot what fine even meant. All of them stared back at me through the mirror. Instead of pushing them away, I had to start saying, "You survived too."

That's what forgiveness looks like at the start. Not excusing or forgetting, but allowing yourself to stop hating survival. Begin a self-forgiveness exercise by standing in front of a mirror each morning or night and saying, "I forgive myself for what I've been through, and I am allowed to heal." Repeat this mantra until it feels more like a step toward peace. Over time, this simple practice can help you reclaim your sense of self.

Some days, the mirror was brutal. I'd see a stranger, a failure, someone unworthy. When self-doubt returned, I learned to acknowledge my feelings and breathe. Setbacks are part of healing. Other days, I caught a glimpse of strength: a fire in my eyes, a body standing firm. Those moments moved me forward.

Eventually, over time, the scar was no longer just a mark in the mirror. It became a story—a transformation of pain into meaning. The scar reminded me that pain may shape you, but it doesn't own you. Survival leaves marks, and those marks can be proof, not shame.

Looking in the mirror, I began to whisper things I didn't fully believe yet:

You are more than what happened to you.

You are not the yelling or the silence.

You are not the bottle or the tie.

You are still here.

You are worthy of love and compassion.

With time and repetition, whispers hardened into ritual. Turning pain into practice, practice into hope. At first, the belief flickered, uncertain, but gradually it grew into the fragile start of becoming someone I no longer had to hide from. To truly channel these whispers into belief, I began a daily practice: each morning, I would stand before the mirror and breathe deeply for ten beats. With each breath, I reminded myself, "I am here. I am strong. I am worthy." This small, repeatable ritual slowly transformed mere words into a powerful belief, bridging the gap between inspiration and action.

"The Scar"

The scar is not the wound.

The scar is the map.

It traces where I've been torn

and points to where I refused to end.

I hated it at first,

But now I read it like scripture:

proof that pain cut deep,

But life cut deeper.

Rebuilding the Soul

Healing isn't magic. It doesn't arrive overnight to sweep everything away. Healing is laborious, slow, chaotic, and draining. It's like that afternoon in the garden, my hands sunk in soil, extracting weeds from neglected corners. The sun pressed on my back, and dirt stained my fingers as I dug, removing debris to nurture new growth. One root stands out: thick, knotted, and so stubborn it seemed to grip the core of the earth. Pulling it loose, I felt a sharp snap—a jolt echoing ruptures in my life. Yet, holding the severed root, I understood that clearing it made space for something new. Healing means rebuilding, piece by piece, even while wounded. Remember, taking your time is valid. Progress is slow, but every small step forward is a real victory on the path to healing.

After the hospital, after the mirror, I realized survival wasn't enough. Breathing kept me alive, but I needed something more. I needed to rebuild the parts of me that had been stripped down by years of yelling, silence, and lies. The soul doesn't patch itself up by accident. To begin, you must take the initiative and start the work yourself.

The first tool was writing. Journaling, if you want to call it that. For me, it was just putting words on paper, so the weight didn't live only inside my chest. Some days, I wrote one sentence: *I'm still here.*

Other days, I poured out pages of memories, questions, curses, and prayers. If you find yourself staring at a blank page, unsure where to start, try beginning with something simple: 'Today I feel…' This gentle prompt can help unlock what's stirring inside you. The truth is, I feared that opening up would mean being swallowed whole by my own darkness, yet the risk of keeping everything bottled up felt greater. The notebook became my second counselor, the one that never interrupted and never judged. It was as if, sometimes, the notebook would reply, "I acknowledge your struggle." This imaginary dialogue was comforting, transforming writing into a shared journey rather than a solitary act.

The second tool was honesty. Real honesty. The kind that felt like ripping skin. I started telling the truth to people, not everyone, but only to those I thought could handle it. My aunt, a counselor, and later, a few friends, who surprised me with their steady hands. Every time I said out loud what I used to keep locked inside, the cry lost some of its grip. In the silence that followed these confessions, I would remind myself to breathe, whispering inwardly, "It's okay to be gentle with yourself." This small act of kindness softened the rawness, offering a calm to the places honesty laid bare.

I understand that not everyone has someone safe and supportive to turn to. In such cases, exploring support groups or helplines can be a vital alternative, offering a space where you can share your truth and find acceptance and understanding. It's important to remember that even if you feel isolated, you're not alone in this journey.

The third tool was discipline. Not punishment, I had endured enough of that. This was self-discipline, the resolve you foster when you choose to fight for yourself. I adopted small rituals that became my allies. Let me describe the rituals that became essential steps in my daily recovery.

"The Sheet Ritual": Waking up and making my bed, even when I didn't want to. The crisp feel of the sheets as my hands smoothed over them grounded me in the present.

- "The Water Choice": Drinking water before I reached for a bottle. The coolness slid down my throat, a tangible reminder of my power to choose renewal in the present. Afterward, I whispered to myself, "Well done." It was a gentle affirmation—a private acknowledgment that small victories, though overlooked, can transform everything.

- "The Cold Walk": Taking walks in the cold, letting air sting my face instead of numbing out with liquor. The crunch of gravel beneath my feet and the rhythm of my breath anchored me in the present moment.

These weren't big victories. Nobody clapped for them. But they stacked up. Each small act was a brick, each sensation a reminder of my resilience. Brick by brick, I started building walls around the parts of me that deserved protection, not punishment. And in the quiet of those moments, when I stood back from my handiwork, I could almost hear the soft nod of approval, like the very walls whispered encouragement, celebrating each small triumph with a silent cheer. With these bricks in place, I discovered that rebuilding required more than discipline—it needed faith.

The fourth tool was faith. Not flawless, not polite, not the kind polished by Sunday-school rhymes and pressed shirts. My faith was unvarnished. Sometimes I shouted at God, demanding answers, but I often met with silence. Yet, in that stillness, one subtle reassurance emerged: the sun, unfailingly rising, hinting at renewal and unseen opportunity each day.

One morning, the dialogue in my mind unfolded like this:

"Why did you let this happen to me?" I shouted into the silence. The emptiness of the room mocked my anger, echoing my doubts with a sterile, indifferent chill.

Then, as I turned away from the window, the light of dawn crept in. A different voice spoke softly, just above a whisper, "See? Another day. Isn't that something?"

In that quiet exchange, there was no grand revelation, just a soft, persistent nudge to look beyond my pain. It was me whispering *help* into the dark and finding, somehow, that I had just enough strength to make it one more day. Faith became a dialogue, not a performance. It gave me permission to believe there was something bigger than my pain.

Rebuilding the soul didn't mean I never fell. I still stumbled. I still drank. I still lied 'I'm fine' when I wasn't. Setbacks were part of the journey, not a sign of my failure. Embracing this notion helped dissolve the shame and replace it with a sense of hope. But the difference was that I now knew there were tools on the table. I knew I could pick up the notebook, the breath, the prayer, the phone. I knew rebuilding wasn't about never breaking again; it was about choosing to rebuild every time I did.

"Brick by Brick"

Not in one day,

not in one miracle.

Brick by brick,

I lay down the pieces.

A sentence.

A breath.

A prayer.

A walk.

My soul is not finished,

But it is no longer rubble.

Dominick Tice

The Pain Was Never Wasted

The echo of a slamming door reverberated through the house, shattering the dawn. I stood, coffee trembling in my hand, each bitter sip a reminder of an existence marred by suffering. For years, I thought my pain was pointless. Every yell thundered in my ears, and every slamming door sent shivers through me. I carried the scars as evidence of a life without purpose. However, Psalm 34:18 reassures us that "The Lord is close to the brokenhearted and saves those who are crushed in spirit." What I didn't realize was that many around me, maybe even those in the same pews at church, silently shared similar scars. This shared weight, though often unspoken, binds us together in our humanity. It wasn't until one morning, in a quiet way, that God made me realize my pain was never wasted.

It wasn't a booming voice or a light show. Instead, it was a shift— a still, patient truth that settled in the hollow places and refused to leave. This realization came slowly: in prayer, in the silence after a church song, or as a scripture line spoke to me in a new way. In those moments, I heard something tender and terrible: what I'd been through could be used. Not to excuse the hurt. Not to hide it. But to turn it into a lantern for someone walking the same dark. If you're in a similar situation, pause and reflect on your experiences in a journal. Write the whispers of your heart and think about what these experiences might mean. Or spend time in prayer, asking for insight and understanding about the role your pain plays in your life. Ask yourself: "Where have I seen God in my pain?" Let this prompt guide your reflection on what these moments might teach you.

God made me see the ledger in a different light. Those tally marks I once read as proof of damage began to read as capacity. Each wound became a place where empathy could live; sleepless nights were classrooms where I learned how to keep growing. Every lie of "I'm fine" taught me how to lead others toward honesty. The pain did not become holy just because it happened; it became useful when I gave it a voice and let God shape it into a testimony. As Romans 8:28 reminds us, "And we know that in all things God works for the good of those who love him, who have been called according to his purpose."

For instance, one day I noticed a friend struggling after a difficult conversation. Rather than brushing it off, I chose to share my own story; as I did, their eyes filled with relief. In that moment, I witnessed the good that can arise from our struggles. Experiences once viewed as suffering have now become a foundation for understanding and purpose.

As you read this, take a moment to pause and reflect on your own body and emotions. What do you feel hearing this story? Where does it resonate within you? Sometimes, our bodies speaks the truths we haven't yet voiced. Allow yourself to listen and be open to what this reflection may reveal about your journey.

When I shared my story, raw and unfiltered, I noticed something happening in the room. Heads bowed not in pity but in recognition. People leaned in because they saw their own reflection in my lines.

For example, a teenager would hear me and say, *"I thought I was alone."* A mother would clutch her child tighter and promise to listen. These reactions helped me understand that God had not let those nights be meaningless. Instead, the pain was a resource—painful, yes, but a resource that could feed someone else's hope.

I understand that sharing your story can be daunting. It's a courageous step that takes time and strength, and it's perfectly okay to begin by taking small steps. Know that you are supported in this journey, and even small acts of sharing can make a significant difference.

I invite you to consider sharing your story. Your words, like stones across a pond, can make ripples of connection and healing. Even your darkest experiences can be a beacon for others. Your vulnerability may lighten your burden and light the path for someone else. What night still echoes in your heart? Your story matters. It can echo back the empathy found here and foster mutual healing.

I don't pretend to know everything. I don't say this to make suffering noble. I just know this: God made a way to redeem what nearly destroyed me. He turned my ledger into a map. In that map, I found purpose. I did not ask for it, but I was given the gift of naming it. Remember: "In the scars of yesterday, find the light for tomorrow."

May those navigating pain find solace in knowing they are not alone. I offer this prayer: May God's presence heal every wound, and may your journey lead to peace. Amen. As you pray, find a quiet space where the gentle light pouring in is accompanied by the rustle of curtains. Feel the exhale of your breath as you release tension. Breathe deeply, and open your hands to receive peace and healing. Let this practice ground the blessing in your life. Additionally, consider reaching out to your local church for support. Many churches offer resources such as pastoral counseling, prayer groups, and support ministries that can provide comfort and guidance. Remember, you are part of a community that cares and is willing to walk with you through difficult times.

"Nothing Wasted"

The wound bled,

The scar stayed,

The story grew.

What I thought was ruin

became a seed.

Every tear,

every scream,

Every night, I begged to end

was folded into soil.

And out of it,

The purpose grew.

Freedom Behind the Flesh

The door slammed shut with a force that echoed through the small room, rattling the bottles lined up like soldiers on the shelf. For so long, I thought freedom meant escape—escape from the yelling, from the silence, from the bottles that represented my struggles, and from the parts of myself I couldn't face. But freedom wasn't about leaving everything behind; it was about choosing to truly live. It meant learning to carry my scars—to bear my past—without letting them drag me under. My healing began with small steps, practical acts like reaching out to someone or finding strength by focusing on the grounding rhythm of my breath, even through the pain.

I once believed my flesh defined me: every bruise, frayed nerve, and the panic sitting in my chest like an anchor that weighed me down. But behind the flesh—behind the visible scars and aches—there was something within me, something God had preserved, unbroken and strong, just waiting to rise.

Freedom didn't arrive all at once. It came in pieces, the same way healing had:

The first time I breathed instead of breaking, relief hummed in my ribs.

The first time I told my story without shame, courage tingled in my fingertips.

The first time I believed God when He whispered, "You *are not wasted, hope blossomed in my chest.*"

The first time I looked in the mirror and saw more than the pain, peace washed over me like a gentle tide.

Freedom looked like forgiveness—not just for others, but for myself. It meant I stopped apologizing for surviving. I used my voice to lift others, rather than hiding behind "I'm fine." A turning point came one day as I sat at the edge of my bed, feeling guilty for the choices I had made when I was in pain. I decided to write a letter to my younger self. In the letter, I admitted my past hurt and confusion and forgave myself for not knowing a better way to cope. Writing allowed me to release some of the burden I was carrying. Through this, I realized my struggles were not mine alone. Many fight these silent battles. In forgiving myself, I found a sense of collective healing—a common humanity that turns personal pain into shared strength.

Freedom looked like faith, a raw faith that said, "*God saw me in the hospital bed, God heard me under the covers, God kept me when I wanted to let go.*" Yet, holding onto faith wasn't always easy. There were moments of doubt, times when I questioned if anyone was listening, if God truly heard my silent cries. These struggles were real, reminding me that doubts are a normal part of the journey. But even as I wrestled with these uncertainties, faith remained a light that refused to let pain be the period at the end of my story. For those who walk different paths of belief, it's important to acknowledge that healing and strength can emerge, irrespective of one's faith or lack thereof. Whether through connections with others, personal reflection, or simply finding moments that bring peace, the journey towards healing is uniquely individual, and all are valid and respected.

Freedom looked like purpose. What once felt like a curse became tools in my hands. My scars became stories. My story became a mirror for others and a window to God's grace.

I won't lie and say freedom means the cry never comes back, or that old temptations never knock. They do. But freedom means I'm no longer chained to them. They knock, and I choose not to open the door, because I'm needed to light another's path. In those difficult moments, I practice grounding myself by focusing on my senses. I take a deep breath, feel my feet firmly on the ground, and count the things I can see, hear, and touch around me. This practice helps anchor me in the present, reminding me that I have the strength to make wise choices. I choose breath. I choose truth. I choose life.

Behind the flesh, behind the pain, behind the scars, there is a freedom nobody can steal, the kind God Himself placed there, waiting for me to step into it. And now, when I speak, I don't just speak for myself. I speak for the child who still hides under covers. I speak for the teen who stares at ceiling fans and wonders if it's worth it. I speak for the adults still numbing themselves because they don't know another way. Remember, you are not alone. Reaching out for support, whether it is a friend, a support group, or seeking professional help, can be a powerful step. Together, we can find hope and forge meaningful connections that light up the path to freedom.

I speak to say: *Freedom is real. And it's waiting for you, too.*

"Behind the Flesh"

The scars remain,

but the chains are gone.

The flesh remembers,

but the soul is free.

God reached into the silence,

took the cry I buried,

and turned it into a song.

Behind the flesh,

I found freedom.

And I will not hide it anymore.

To the One Still Struggling

This book wasn't easy to write, and I know it wasn't easy to read. But I need you to hear me clearly: if you are holding on by a thread, you are not alone. Remember, it is okay to reach out for immediate help. Contact a crisis helpline or support network, as they are designed to provide you with the guidance and support you need.

I know what it's like to cry yourself to sleep. I know what it's like to hide behind "I'm fine" until the words taste like ash. I know the urge to tie a knot or stare at a ceiling fan, wondering if anyone would notice if you were gone. I know how pain drowns in bottles, lies, and silence.

But I also know this: God can turn the ugliest nights into something more. He took my pain—the yelling, the silence, the scars—and showed me it wasn't wasted. He showed me my breath has a purpose. Freedom was waiting, even when I couldn't see it.

If you're reading this and feel unheard, I hear you. Your cry matters. Your scars matter. Your survival matters. You are not invisible.

You don't need to have everything figured out or fix everything now. Start small. Take one breath. Write one line. Tell one person the truth. Pray one prayer, even if it's just, *God, help me.* Listen to a peaceful song, step outside to enjoy the sunlight, or call a helpline for support. Each small step counts.

Don't let silence deceive you. Don't let shame say you're unworthy. Your presence, reading these words, means your story isn't over. More is yet to be written.

The road won't always be easy. But you don't have to walk it alone. God is with you, and so are people like me—people with scars, who know the cry, who found light through cracks and didn't let the dark win. Reach out to a support group, helpline, or trusted person. Communities and individuals are eager to lend a hand and offer support.

Your pain does not define you. Your scars don't disqualify you. Your survival isn't an accident.

Keep breathing. Keep fighting. Keep living. There is freedom waiting for you beyond physical and emotional struggles. This freedom is about finding peace within yourself, recognizing your worth, and embracing the possibilities that life has to offer.

With love, truth, and hope,

Dominick Tice

Resources

If you are struggling with suicidal thoughts or mental health challenges, please know there is help. You matter, and support is available. United States:

• Suicide & Crisis Lifeline: Dial or text 988 (24/7, free, confidential)

• Veteran Crisis Line: Dial 988 then press 1 or text 838255

• National Alliance on Mental Illness (NAMI): 1-800-950-NAMI

• Crisis Text Line: Text HOME to 741741. Other countries: search for international crisis helplines to find support near you. You deserve help.

Faith & Encouragement:

• Psalm 34:18 "The Lord is close to the brokenhearted and saves those who are crushed in spirit."

• Jeremiah 29:11 "For I know the plans I have for you," declares the Lord, "plans to prosper you and not to harm you, plans to give you hope and a future."

Or if you just need a listening ear or a shoulder to cry on, so you don't have to keep it bottled up, text, call, or leave me a voicemail, and I will be your support. YOU MATTER! (314) 325-2640

You are not alone.

Reach out.

Breathe.

Live.